WHO IS A DAISY GIRL SCOUT?

Girl Scouts of the U.S.A.
420 Fifth Avenue
New York, N.Y. 10018-2702

GIRL SCOUTS OF THE U.S.A.

B. LaRae Orullian, *National President*
Mary Rose Main, *National Executive Director*

Inquiries related to the *Who Is a Daisy Girl Scout?*
storybook should be directed to Program,
Girl Scouts of the U.S.A., 420 Fifth Avenue,
New York, N.Y. 10018-2702.

Author
Martha Jo Dennison

Contributor
Candace White Ciraco

Designer
Kaeser and Wilson Design Ltd.

Illustrator
Kristin Goeters

Printed in the United States of America

ISBN   0-88441-276-8

10   9   8   7   6   5   4   3   2   1

Who is that girl they're all talking about?
Why, don't you know?
She's a Daisy Girl Scout.

That Daisy is honest—she knows
what is true.

She tries to be fair when she's
playing with you.

She helps where she's needed—
she'll get the job done.

She's happy and cheerful
to everyone.

She's friendly and kind
whenever she's out,

and acts like a sister to
every Girl Scout.

She listens to parents and
leaders as well.

She tries not to be wasteful and
that you can tell.

She takes care of her world and
gives back what it needs.

She shows others she cares through
her words and her deeds.

Now you don't have to wonder
who that Daisy can be.
You knew all along that Daisy is ME!

THE GIRL SCOUT PROMISE

On my honor, I will try:
To serve God and my country,
To help people at all times,
And to live by the Girl Scout Law.

THE GIRL SCOUT LAW

I will do my best:
to be honest
to be fair
to help where I am needed
to be cheerful
to be friendly and considerate
to be a sister to every Girl Scout
to respect authority
to use resources wisely
to protect and improve the world around me
to show respect for myself and others through
my words and actions

The Story of Juliette Low

Girl Scouts of the U.S.A.
420 Fifth Avenue
New York, N.Y. 10018-2702

GIRL SCOUTS OF THE U.S.A.

B. LaRae Orullian, *National President*
Mary Rose Main, *National Executive Director*

Inquiries related to *The Story of Juliette Low*
should be directed to Program,
Girl Scouts of the U.S.A., 420 Fifth Avenue,
New York, N.Y. 10018-2702.

Author
Martha Jo Dennison

Contributor
Candace White Ciraco

Designer
Kaeser and Wilson Design Ltd.

Illustrator
Frank Steiner

Printed in the United States of America

ISBN   0-88441-276-8

10   9   8   7   6   5   4   3   2   1

The Story of Juliette Low

Juliette Gordon Low was born a long time ago in Savannah, Georgia. When she was just a baby, her uncle said she was going to be a daisy. He knew she was special. So, everyone called her Daisy from then on.

When Daisy was young, she liked to play with her brothers, sisters, and cousins and climb trees, take care of animals, and go exploring.

She also liked to write
stories and plays and act
them out. She liked to draw

pictures, tell jokes, and

start and run clubs.

So, you see, Daisy could do
many things.

Daisy loved animals so much that once she saved a kitten from drowning in a flood. Another time she placed her mother's quilt over a cow so it wouldn't get cold in the middle of the night. Well, her mother was not happy because the cow trampled the quilt! Daisy thought the cow needed the quilt to keep warm, but it really didn't. It was fine in the stable.

Daisy had animals around her whenever she could. She had dogs, birds, and other animals as pets throughout her life. They made her happy and she took good care of them.

As Daisy grew up, she had problems with her ears. She often got bad ear infections. When she got married to Willy Low, a piece of rice landed in her ear and made her hearing worse. Daisy never let her problems stop her from doing things and always kept trying.

Daisy and Willy never had any children. They lived in England and Scotland for many years. Daisy was always doing things. She even made her own iron gate for her house.

After Willy died, Daisy kept learning new things and meeting people. Her friends, Lord Baden-Powell and his sister Agnes, told her about the Boy Scouts and Girl Guides they had started. Daisy thought that was a great idea!

Daisy decided to start troops for girls in the United States. On March 12, 1912, the first Girl Scout troops were started in Savannah, Georgia. That's why March 12 is the Girl Scout birthday.

Soon there were Girl Scouts all over the country. Today, millions of girls ages 5 through 17 or in grades kindergarten through 12 who accept the Girl Scout Promise and Law are Girl Scout members. Even though Daisy died a long time ago, in 1927, we still remember her. Daisy liked to have fun, to make things, to have adventures, to help people, and to take care of animals. Best of all, she started Girl Scouts in the United States. Daisy really was special. And so are you, because you're a Daisy Girl Scout too!